the heart is a holding

lateisha davine lovelace-hanson

Burning Eye

Burning Eye Books
Never Knowingly
Mainstream

Copyright © 2025 Lateisha Davine Lovelace-Hanson

The author asserts the moral right under the Copyright, Designs and Patents Act 1988 to be identified as the author of this work.

All rights reserved. No part of this publication may be reproduced, stored in a retrieval system, or transmitted, in any form or by any means without the prior written consent of the author, nor be otherwise circulated in any form of binding or cover other than that in which it is published and without a similar condition being imposed on the subsequent purchaser.

This edition published by Burning Eye Books 2025

"Ever New" Words and Music by Beverly Glenn-Copeland copyright ©1986, Reproduced by permission of Third Side Music Inc

Cover design by Meera Shakti Osborne
Cover Photograph by Shannay Nia Henry-Brown

www.burningeye.co.uk

@burningeyebooks

Burning Eye Books
15 West Hill, Portishead, BS20 6LG

ISBN 978-1-913958-42-8

Contents

To Do List	4
end of the world smoke alchemy	5
if Beverly Glenn-Copeland wrote future a song, it'll be enough. it'll be plenty. it'll be Ever New.	6
you want to write a joy poem	7
wi reach	8
A Radical Dharma	9
Eye + Eye	10
how i eat mango	12
Clarity Conditioning: a love letter to heal from harm	14
dis(dawtah)order	15
~ the dedication of returned breath ~	17
don't get me wrong, you're still a dick	18
the journey of Aji the sweet pepper	19
metaphors for a Black future // part 1 // well de memory came	21
metaphors for a Black future // part 2 // wi aks well?	21
AFTER DE MEADOW //	22
AFTER DE READING //	23
space-holding futurism / how long we been together	24
ally pally afropunk 2016 (&) last words my friend ever got to say to me	25
Until This Moon Night	26
Enabling Trans(a)gressions	28
Working title (a coming out story)	29
Abolition Is Your Ocean Calling	30
love letter to a real one in apocalypse	31
THE GREETING // for when it's all said and done	32
To Do List	33

To Do List

- wake
- be
- intention: brave this new-old
- world into view. let
- go well. find others. create
- bridges.
- be
- rest

end of the world smoke alchemy

burning is how end begins
crackle is how we choose avant-new
belonging through papaya smoke reach
bashment fire riddims

her prayer become dark fruit fantasy & her gods become beckon
she break borders, delectable destruction
blackstrap map, iridescent skin

a child of creation frees what must be told
a free child creates what must be told of
a creation told child what must be of free

through burn & papaya smoke dawn bruk

    wi bun dis ting dung tuh di ground

        ((tell dem!))

            at end begins
                at gods become beckon
                    at smoke dawn

bruk

                        we be

alchemy

if Beverly Glenn-Copeland wrote future a song, it'll be enough. it'll be plenty. it'll be Ever New.

cake walk across time's brink
search sound
systems of built belonging
play mas sunday mawning, converse with carnival
turned apocalypse autumn, ruptures modulate
you are new to this 4-beat season

welcome the spring, the summer rain
softly turn, to sing again

on repeat refuge
unchord yourself from spiral time
chew yam and green banana verses
break down

welcome the bud
the summer blooming flower

gather godplanets, be beside
yourself, feel red
let all weight blanket

welcome the child whose hand i hold
welcome to you, both young and old

record your father, in whispered homecoming: *teisha*
i never knew i was
so loved. on hearing, you return to daughter
present him a story, til both of you are golden
prayer

we, are
ever   new

you want to write a joy poem

but your death keeps coming
boils the kettle when no one asked for tea
silently opens windows when winter waits outside
refuses bedtime when tomorrow is planned

it is hard for you
to write a joy poem
when death demands
peppermint tea & blasts of fresh air lullaby

your death daydreams
bounces in denim dungarees, plants trees at break
reimagines clapping songs, and keeps pocketfuls of too many
wise beyond her years

your death wants hugs, you death wants apology
follows you with a playground of questions
dances to s club 7 and knows how secrets take root in hidden
builds dens out of cardboard summer and family absence
scuffed knees and years missing
speaks to rainbows as if they are ducks, deer and hauntings

your death is here
soft-cheeked, rope-skipping
tickle belly laughing
waiting for you to write them in

wi reach

maybe it's ridiculous
to love
maybe we just met
in this lifetime
maybe this feeling
is elder
tree enough
a bloom beyond
words become matterless
tomorrow wills action
i arrive into your unfolded presence
maybe i can rest the lie of
unworthiness in your swimmer arms
maybe i can't
write the unending need
stories without name
maybe it's all ready
written in dream
maybe the vision
spoken is a more-than maybe
we will turn soil
grow or decay
move earth together along coastal path
maybe he will be our young one
desiring a body to be made
maybe all that's unmade is returning to a future
one that comes lightly in resurrected breath
maybe desire is silly is solstice is airbnb-ing til mawning
to be open heart yes, in mum's place, earls court
migraine-fuelled, moonlight, single bed sex
maybe we medicine
something playful unlost
maybe wi
alive to this?

A Radical Dharma

i don't wanna do well in the institution
this is a sign of sickness imo

i wanna do sick in community
this is a sign of wellness imo

i know which one i've chosen
this is a sign of revolutionary love imo

behind the word 'success' there is a practice. inside practice is a choice

Eye + Eye

girl
you know you a seer
iris of failed perfection
keeper of two worlds
split countries cradle your face to see
meteor, see colour sky, see silence
screaming
rum thick with ancestral flight

we ascend your calabash mouth
we banana leaf your liberated shadow
we are your unseen smile

we two anointing
we two sananga track
we two tiger i + i

reject frames that do not work
break the way your mother ripped off your child face
stamped back into sand

see we you

blessed you with cited refusals
stitched into lineage reckonings
no loose knowing
no pattern out of our sight
trust, another way of world is a coming
is a time
is a open
the tried parts of you
unhide
have you seen yourself

the way we do?

everytime you mirror
reflection
beautifully cracked

we face, you
fruit-filled + fragmented
felt
i + i = child

how i eat mango

mum always knew how to get the most succulent fruit home
how to press
her heart in each squeeze
> *the top and bottom, teish, will tell you if it's ripe…*
> *press gently, but press firm, feel how soft it can be*

knowing mango was her way
> *find the soft, if it's there, it's ours*

to cut home open. on a plastic sun
rise plate. mum makes me a mountain
> *aahhh, memory, it smell sweet*

i gap-tooth chew
chase each chunk down my saturday morning stomach
ignore fibres trapped. as summer stains
joy drip down the horizon hug of my chest
i am belly full with excited wanting
> *slow down, savour it, smell so sweet*

mum always knew. how to press. find the soft
> *teish, leave the seed flesh for me*

between memory flavoured wanting. i vision her as a little one
holding dear mango in her hands
through seasons of family leaving like domino. for a better life
ina h'ingland
and an older brother who fell. from the family mango tree
sent him searching Jamaica's estranged streets
> *juiciest, but hardest part*

i see her sticky waving goodbyes. dressed in cotton white socks
and pinafore brave blue. plaited hair tied
in ribbon purple protection. grown
from Xaymaca's Taíno African seed skin. mango
made mum fleshy
made mum skip
made mum sing
> *brown girl in de ring tralalalala*
> *there's a brown girl in de ring traalalalalala*
> *there's a brown girl in de ring tralalalala*
> *and she looks like a sugar in a plum plum plum*

beneath her feet she runs
wild. over unmarked graves and maddened seed
purple ribbon bare. white socks brown girl blue. she climbs
to pick fresh before others
fall. yes. she bites straight in di story outta wi
ah tayse mi muss protect. sweet memory pon mi lips

Clarity Conditioning: a love letter to heal from harm

to make *fuck you!* feelings, holy again
is to recognise, the myriad ways you came
for my flesh
under sacrificial confusion, you are
less victim, more wolf, more sheep in youth clothing

                                                               do you

to make *fuck you!*
i make map of enclosed wounds, the abandon
of my neckthroat holy again
leaving skeletal trails of tasteless gourd, damp scent
of unfiltered tobacco tinted by unresolved rescues, you
folded bombs into future details

                                                  have a sense

to make feelings
i endure time
-lapse
fuck you! is recollect reckoning, to speak holy from my breast
is to see it coming, is to remember structural reproduction
is to say
what day it is
three years full of belly bloat
and five hundred years' service to *other*
samhain 31/10/24. the morning after. purge deep, purge well

                                       of what this feeling needs?

to make *fuck you!* feelings holy
is odyssey / between love and extraction /
care and harm / travelling what is / said and done is to / feel /
is to feel undone

                        what this vulnerable part wants to say?

8-legged wild one
root roaming ancestor wood, make feast of fire, please i need
protection

    eco-therapist: do you have a sense of what this feeling needs? what this
                                     vulnerable part wants to say?

dis(dawtah)order

liberation nah dun
the did we a dun nuh

   she mix
   she play gift   she
                         she Black children re-raised by night
                            –
                         she
                  sweet homing
                  duppy talking
                  Beloved killing
                  she is as Sethe writ, she is as Toni knew
                        –

may we befriend the 4C of time

return blue magic   initiation of wanting   to curl back into original

form
–
wake gasping
                wake half eaten   wake drenched
                                            just / wake
                                                       –

                                  di family
                                        left
                                              in pain

passage
        of feeling
                it just life   –
                                  traverse mother
                                  butterfly hug
                                  head hold
                                  tension release
                                  an opened eye

                                        belief that you can
                                        stop her sea moss
heart
                                        from irregular beats
—

generation confessions
dat you *are* her
salvation
dat dawtah who ran
                    until atoms split

                                        until dutch pot and
                                        fantasy full

        until mama recipes run down yuh
        until saltfish scotch bonnet golden gate yuh

                            until
                    surrender conjures
        stop sufferation
                    contracted collapse
        starburst contemplation
                all within you

~ the dedication of returned breath ~

did you know it was me
coming with bone-water griefs? pockets of protective yarrow
propranolol and prayer. hoping to release trapped moths
stuffed up my stomach-mouth

did you know i'd come, baring hallowed guava
gifts to mourning rising? of how many
clingfilmed years it's taken our inner young ones
to play out here. beyond boundaries of loss knowing

did you know i was reopening
my aorta again? here, in spring's wake of live-death
countless edge enforced skins, shed. decluttered chest
sounding no mores

what goes unsaid and unseen you knew
from the very first cut of hearing
what it would take
for me to hold you

i fear the hunter's moon
orbiting the flashlights lodged
in your slot machine eyes

shadows teased by echo
~~'i love you'~~
~~'i see you'~~
~~'i am here'~~

i trace neon blue
my fingers two-step the exposed
bridge of your arms, dancing
borderlines, disappearing red

i stir toward your skin
offer myself back to sand dune
chest, deer alert, is a wordless
mountain turned on

i stay ~~here?~~ as we strip
        search, yawn risk
            you bristle sweep my
                temple, bonesoft with
                        sorry
                        caressing
                            the land
                                of my
                                  lips

don't get me wrong, you're still a dick

the journey of Aji* the sweet pepper

you were handed to me to be washed under water

taking away your hard
armoured chemical glaze of others'
touch you did not ask for

all tight red skin and dimples
hanging off your mother's stem
waiting young
will the ripe moments
fall?

interrupted, you were picked
into a box

shipped across geologies of origin

changed sun passed around, purchased
secateurs to mother, tongue
renamed *capsicum annum*
you are categorised, sorted

you were handed to me water to be washed under

is your blood-red
born again as new fruit
cut insides, splayed flesh
our seeds
unsaved

how many ways can i slice you?
make grief from your form?
i asked him, he said *strips*

you were me handed to me, water under water, washed

---
* Aji: Taíno indigenous Jamaican word for peppers.

your death is more side order than what came before or after
you the fullest course, generations grew
to ask how you like soil, sown
names, ceremony

you watched hands change
confining perennial cycles into doors
deep horizon
inside fractured into annual uprootings

yet here you *are*, my friend
ways many, teaching grow, teaching hands, teaching

journey

metaphors for a Black future // part 1 // well de memory came

definitions of the word 'well' from merriam-webster english language dictionary // **fi wi well demand wi own definitions**
1. *to rise to the surface and usually flow forth //* **dis**
2. *a pit or hole sunk into the earth to reach a supply of water //* **inna invitation**
3. *a source from which something may be drawn as needed //* **go dung deh so**
4. *to an extent approaching completeness //* **tru de sacred**
5. *completely cured or healed //* **powa of wata**

metaphors for a Black future // part 2 // wi aks well?

how do we

honour: waters of unended mournings
                breathe: cascades of transoceanic memory
birth: ourselves into dignified deaths
                undrown: channels to reach storybook surface
well up: release soca siren seas

                      we want
                      to break
                      get free
                      stay well
            at the same damn
                      of time

                      mama?
                                        ah dis a funeral rite
      ah dis de way

                  yuh rise?

AFTER DE MEADOW //

a meadow met me in croydon
peering beyond, a saving sun
invited me to take
his pink, purpling out day

you have my aunt's face

smoke ghost and healing
grass, seed hold me
to sing the endless stages
of Grandad's name

Lloyd
Joel
Ludlow
Lovelace

over and over, over and over, over
and over, until cow and fox and
snake came home
grateful, to finally
be gifted a meadow song

and her ways. she was a healer

it was *only* then
grief had a re-sounding last
name for vessel, alive my ache
seer, descending light

she found me

with sorrel-stained hands
they came
with ankara cloth selfies

>   she came
> with needing more time, before ride train home
>   I came here to cry

AFTER: *You have my aunt's face, Teisha, and her ways. She was a healer. She found me*

AFTER DE READING //

what Dad said
after my reading at Grandad's
funeral

> *you was like a river, Teisha*
>   *flowing. no banks*
> *no nothing*
> *a river, running free*

I had to unleash the door of my back
set us free, always
and *only* to hold the hands
of our dead

space-holding futurism / how long we been together

present tense unfoldings, your arms branch
deepknowingforgivenesstrust across the sixteen-year-old brink
of my back
my right cheek surrenders yeslovesure to your shoulder
teenage, we the height
of father sky resolve

i want to squeeze you so tight our atoms fuse together

you usher undiluted incantation
stability's libation call
drinking rupture, density of lifetimes
towards repair
towards sweat salutation peppermint bed kissed mornings
towards pound shop painted birthday decorations, blu-tacked
over mould-stained london wall rentings

together i want
our atoms to fuse
squeeze you
so tight

pulling me closer
generations of joy awaken
space held open, we breathe slow free fast
sensations bloom unruly shapes
of repatterned commitment
possibilities, we play

together   fuse atoms   our tight   so you squeeze   to want i

in the park before youth theatre / huddersfield town centre / spring 2006

ally pally afropunk 2016 (&) last words my friend ever got to say to me

You: I'll be right back

my friend lives at the bottom of our london lungs
give space to praise, we make-believe belong

I'll be back right

we trust dark sky edge, resting homeland of our tonight
purpose this city with broken hearts

I'll be alright

we embrace bassline into living ambit, Cakes da Killa soon come
trails of mirrordark bodies, skank whine bruk cosmology
reclamation sun

right back I'll be

we rum sacrifice shame, forgive ghosts of missing
calls and texts unread, pray to not leave it too long

I'll be
back

to rite?
a phone call
you getting your kitchen, hallway and bathroom done
me moving to a new address
we are still layers coming undone
you clear the dust off your walls
we plan our next gallery outing, celebrate, repeat
two blue ticks
a phone call

your mum, the answering

london lungs edge rest tonight, in broken heart bassline bodies, ghosts
and i wish, so hard, that you could come *right back*

Until This Moon Night

•|•

pelvis in prayerful push
gully legs widened
she de open
channel of two
demanding earthside
birthing, baby
twins, fire ready to be, Born Free
Great Grandmother Amy
clay of lunar passage ways
was thirty-five

                         when death
                         broke in

   (•)   •

(this baby)   delivered in   Amyandthisbaby
flames   Amy's final   heldwaterclose fought
breath   broke the bind   wanted deserved tried
oh baby found first breath   life life life taken ohmama
oh baby survived   cry ohhowdeath brokein
            oh baby lived   ohthe9nights oh stillness oh
(this baby)heldwaterclose   mama ohflames Amy
stirred sleep   andthisbaby died
crytomakeitthrough   throughash
crythrough   ash
          absorbcharcoalsplitwaters
             her moon, belly
              cleared night

•=•

she Jamaican
Arawak-Taíno African-Ashanti
european –
out of many, one peoples
six children and a country undoing
wood water and blood
mothers and children are kidnapped in my family
women, mediums of medicinal bravery

•••

                        she wanted me
        living refusal of control, a transgression
           i live by loving the ways i do

<•>

i am
        thirty-five
dreaming
        of birthing
a wanted, a welcomed, a you are mine child
        fortified, lullabied
i wake
        to swallowed metal, the *four times more likely to…*[**]
transporting me
                                            to Amy
                                            to the Other Side

no   •
 i did not know   •
  know i did not   •
   know what happened   •
    i did not know what happened   •
     what happened to Great Grandmother Amy i did not know •

Until This Moon Night
                                            Great Grandmother Amy
                     mi know
                        •

She and her Baby are freeing the newborn sound of mango tree
    with sun shaking salt soil sweetness, such holy lands
                        of the dead

and in this telling   Amy
                         and her baby   *Live*

               •••
                •

[**] 'British Black women die in childbirth at an appalling rate. I'm tired of fighting a racist system in vain'. Candice Brathwaite, *The Guardian,* 20 April 2023

Enabling Trans(a)gressions

sometimes love comes / from crossing borders / the leap of faith is a trusted ancestor wanting you to survive / when we say the word trans, the first place my bodymind goes is the *transatlantic trade of...* i need you to know this. i need you. i / sometimes / when there is a mind there is an unsafe place. my therapist threw a lifeline wi dis / wake with the birds and remember my calling is theirs, something you have to wake up first / listen / sometimes there can only be an *always*

Working title (a coming out story)

cum closer you
deity deep tongue
taste-talking
fugitive feminisms
into my 2am
languished body
ache orgasm
bruk back
bruk out goddess
turning returning
snake skin magic
fertile ground cove
deep penetration
you got moves
sea soaking
feel home-hug
cum closer you
concentrated essence
rose water primal bonnet-off passion
deep well
water fun
freedom song
straddle rider
turn me out

forgotten gods are turning and returning
to pleasure dome

For the gentle ones   I go to bed I go to sleep better   for knowing you are here in the world   For knowing you are there   In this world   For knowing when alarm bells ring   seen and unseen You come with rosemary hawthorn lemongrass   You come with shea butter hands Veil thin Yes Welcome Kisses on the forehead   Gulfs so deeply held   We oceans know your name   We oceans *thank you*   We oceans know breakdown breakthrough break Free Sinking sea depths of fear hidden*owed*BreatheKeepbreathing breathe   your way   through memory

Abolition Is Your Ocean Calling

love letter to a real one in apocalypse

my friend
the starched night is ending
unresolved & held

                stare into this open secret
                & breathe thrice again

                                rest assured you did
                                not turn to stone

THE GREETING // for when it's all said and done

who speaks through a mouth?
who says *i*
see you
who says *hey* looking through and
into my eyes
for tidal voice that speaks surrender
into open pores and a hairy top lip
into grey hairs and chipped front teeth
who speaks back
this comfort of thirty-two summers

that I   am alive
that I   have made it this far
that I   am miracle
that I   am dreamvision
that I   survived
that I   speak tenderness for
you   to come back…

to mushroom trip wheat meadow and burst banks of your sex legs
to universe unbound by cold water dips reaching Oshun feet
to forest you laid on top of your back — both of you wept
a door creaked
a sunset grieved
who is it that knew
the righteousness of screaming into a lake

someone must say *hey*
to the done and wordless

who is it that makes ghosts gone
to let joy return to space in my chest
when I emailed five therapists today
when I couldn't get out of bed
when all I could see was my own reflection
who is it that says *hey*
with a smile
cos I   made it thru this day

To Do List

- ~~wake~~
- ~~be~~
- ~~intention. brave this new-old~~
- ~~world into view. let~~
- ~~go well. find others. create~~
- ~~bridges.~~
- ~~be~~
- rest

Born in London to Jamaican parents, **Lateisha Davine Lovelace-Hanson** is an interdisciplinary artist, writer, nature practitioner, social justice facilitator and somatic therapist. Their writing has been shared across the UK and internationally, including with Montez Press and Radio, V&A Museum, Bethlem Gallery, Camden Art Centre, Queer Ecologies Festival, Free Word, Wort Journal, Skew: Black Embodiment,]performance s p a c e[, Artsadmin's Apocalypse Reading Room, resting up collective, Southbank Centre, The Albany and For Books' Sake.

Lateisha's plays include A Tree, S/He Breathe/S, well de memory came and De Original Sound, with work produced by Raze Collective and Stanley Arts. Lateisha's film The Gift - was selected for LADA Screens. They are a Roundhouse and Hammer & Tongue poetry slam finalist, and an alumnus of Obsidian Foundation, Apples and Snakes' Writing Room and Soho Theatre Writers' Lab.

Acknowledgements

Water, earth, sky and ancestors for holding me through this book. To the fire: you cleared the path.

Thank you, Beverly Glenn-Copeland, my north star and Toni Morrison, for Beloved. Those who helped me trust again: Lama Rod Owens (and retreat community), Leila Sadeghee, Mina Aidoo, Jo Miller, Chand and Hackney City Farm BIPOC eco-therapy group, therapists Eve and Rachel, and long COVID specialist, Dr Joshi.

Gratitude to: Sanah Ahsan, Victoria Adukwei Bulley and Hasti for your encouraging editorial insights. Thank you Burning Eye Books. To SHED and Thirty Percy for resourcing this work. To Jack and the Leo & Friends community. Thank you Jean 'Binta' Breeze, Warsan Shire, Inua Ellams and Jacob Sam-La Rose for your formative workshops. Scottish BPOC Writers Network for your invitation to facilitate on 'Metaphors For A Black Future'.

My parents Maxine Joy Lovelace and Linton Roy Hanson. You are so loved. My siblings, here, afar, dead and alive: Desreen, Jasmin, Kim, Jason and Jonny.

Sacred Circle collective: Tommy, Zahra and Anna. To Caroline, Giselle, Delwyn, Amarnah, Shannay, Ged, Dré, Naomi and Carmina. Access assistants; Yasmyn, Princess and Cecilia. And you, Brian Appiah Obeng. S – you are in these words. To Kes, you're a mountain of enduring love.

Thank you, reader. For being my witness.

www.ingramcontent.com/pod-product-compliance
Ingram Content Group UK Ltd.
Pitfield, Milton Keynes, MK11 3LW, UK
UKHW011056021225
465586UK00007B/87